This Coloring Book

Belongs to:

_____

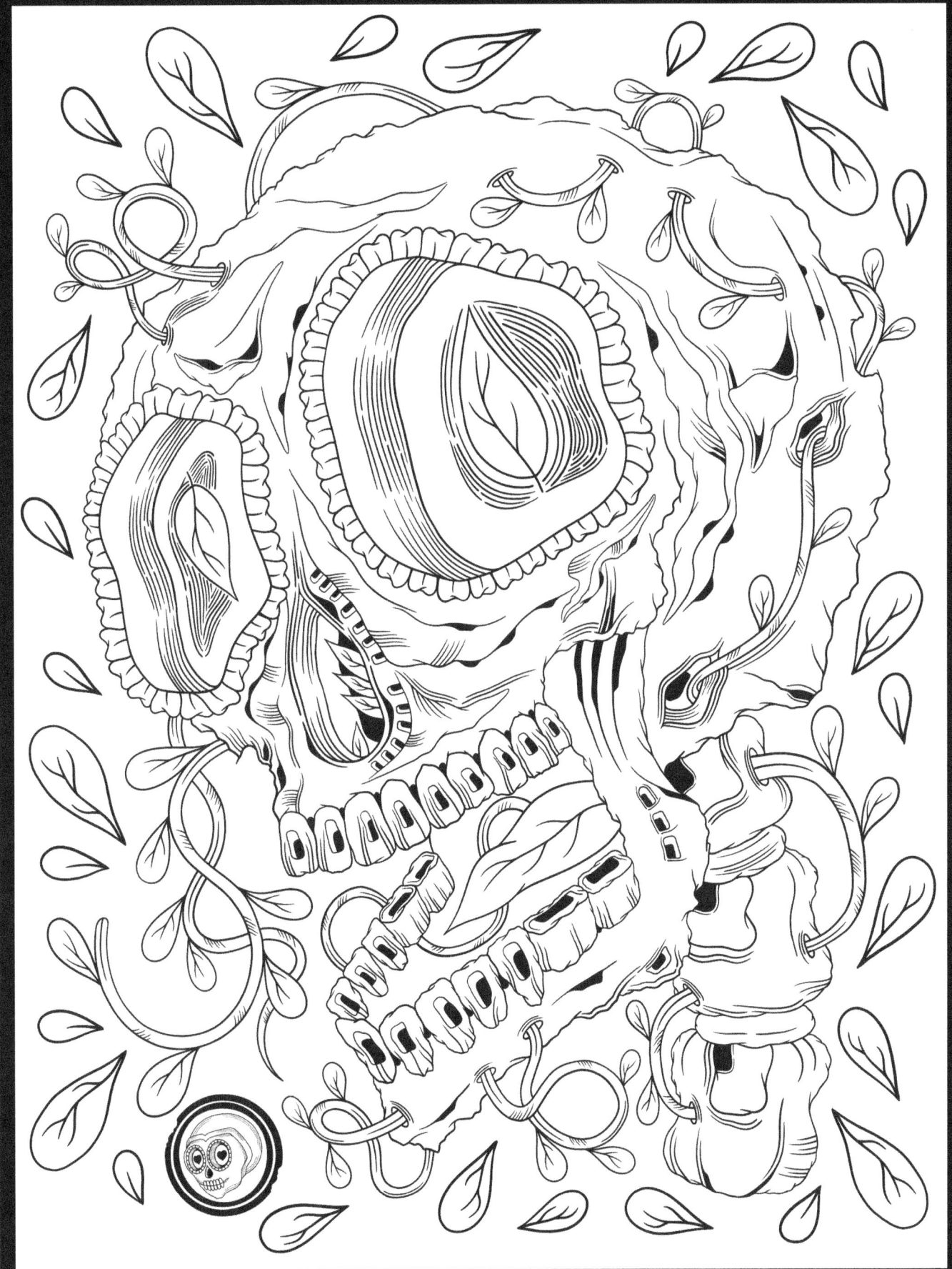

The Colors of Fall

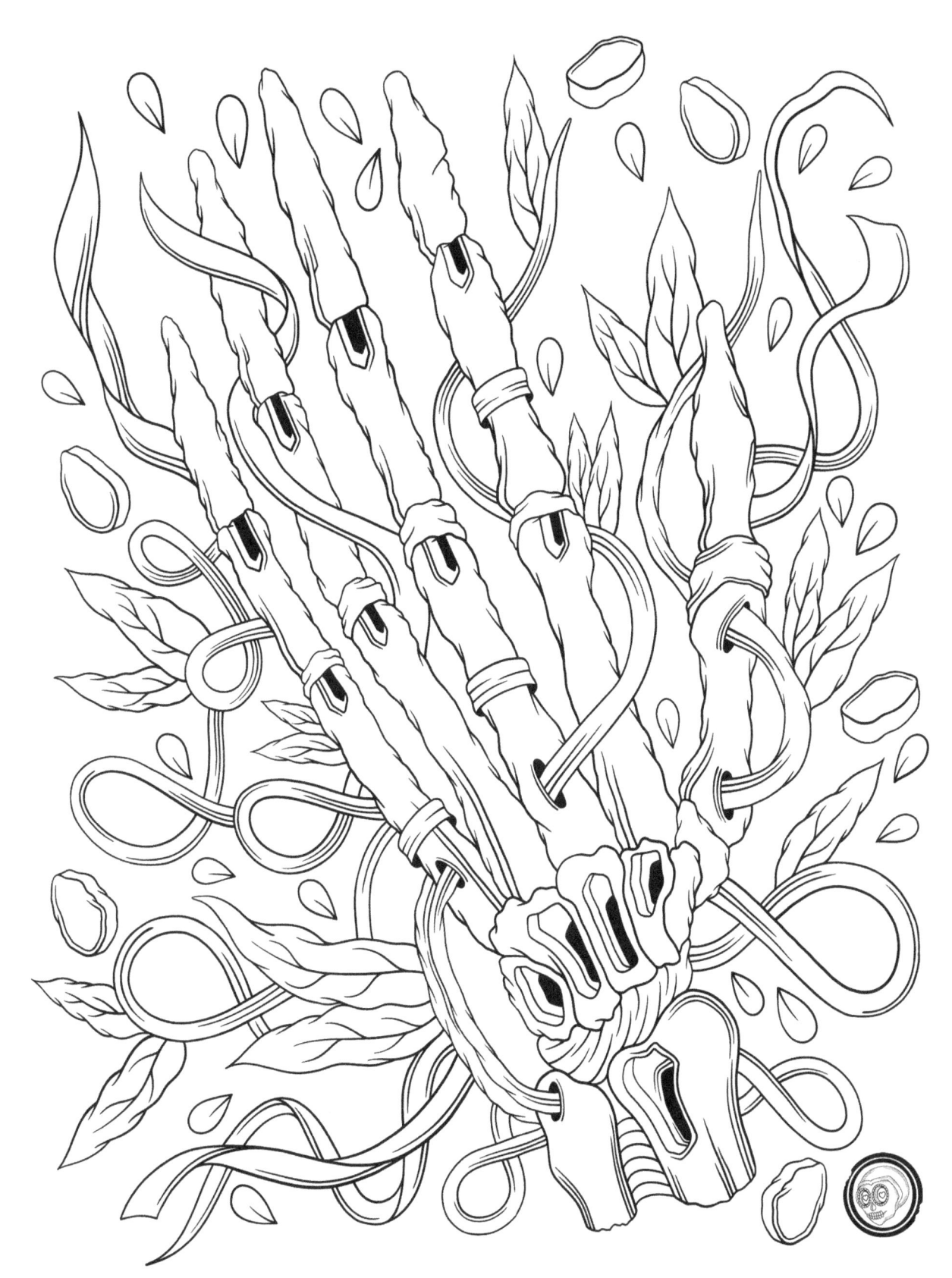

The Hand n Nature

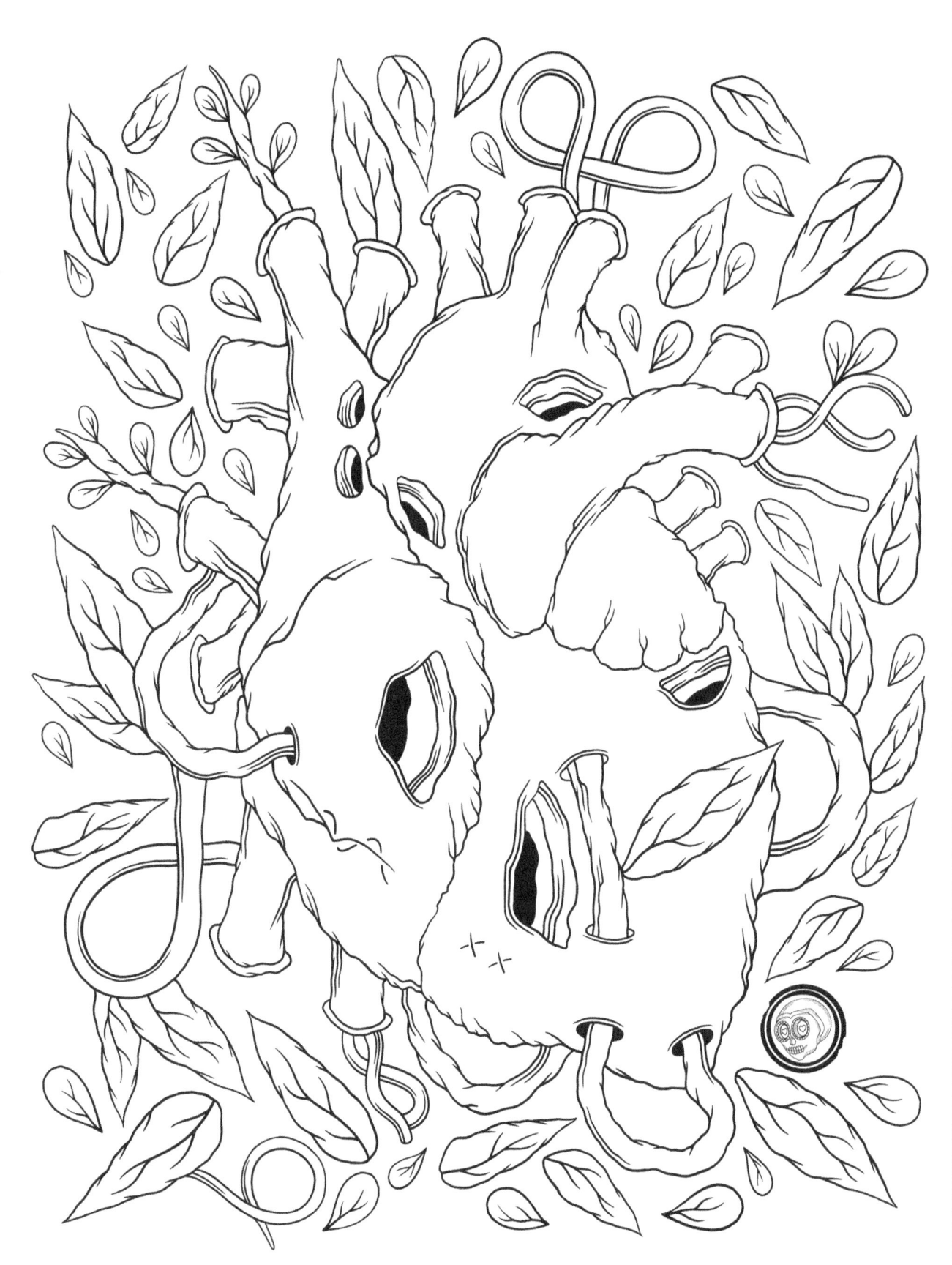

The Love Of Nature

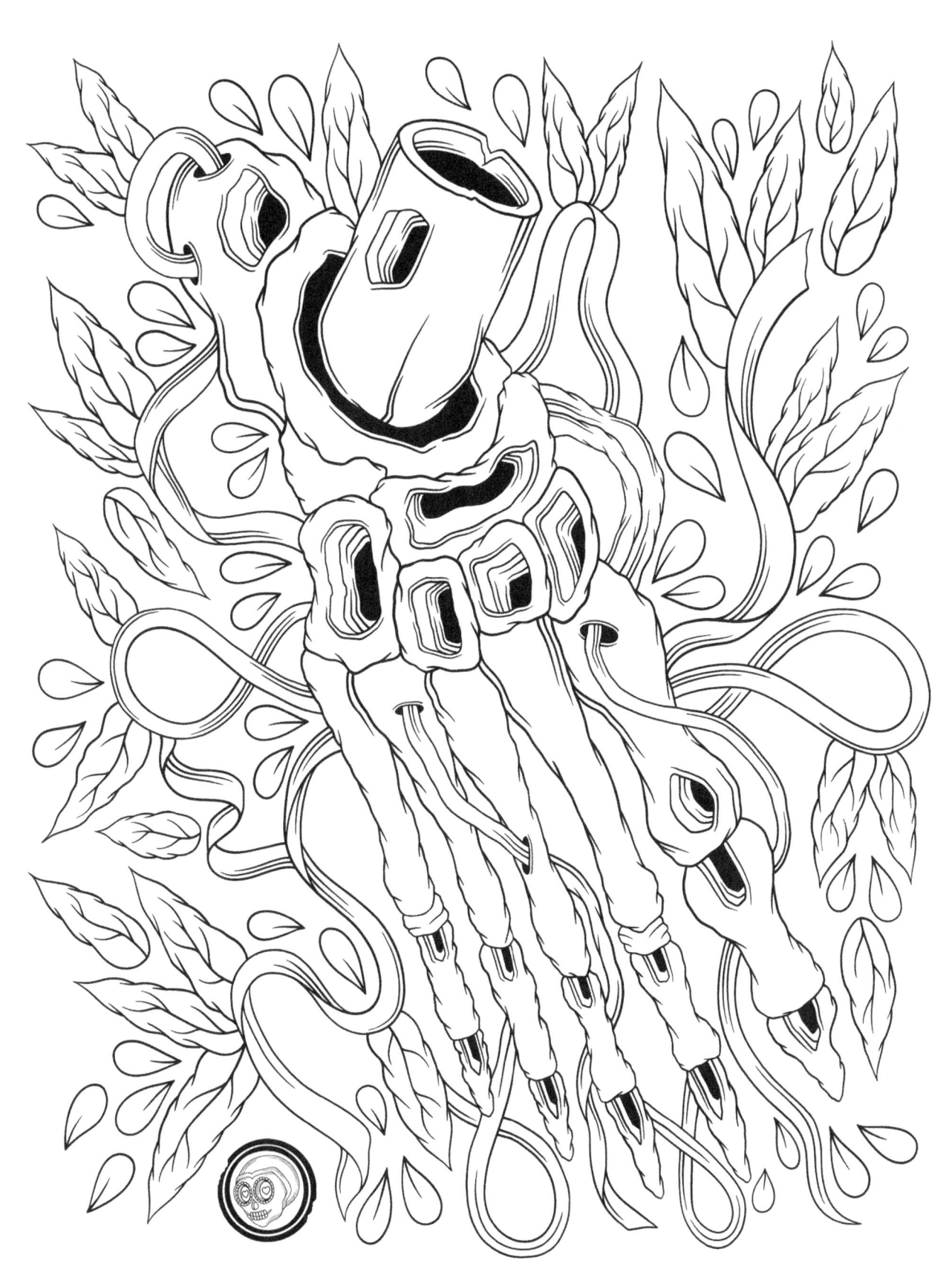

The Foot n Nature

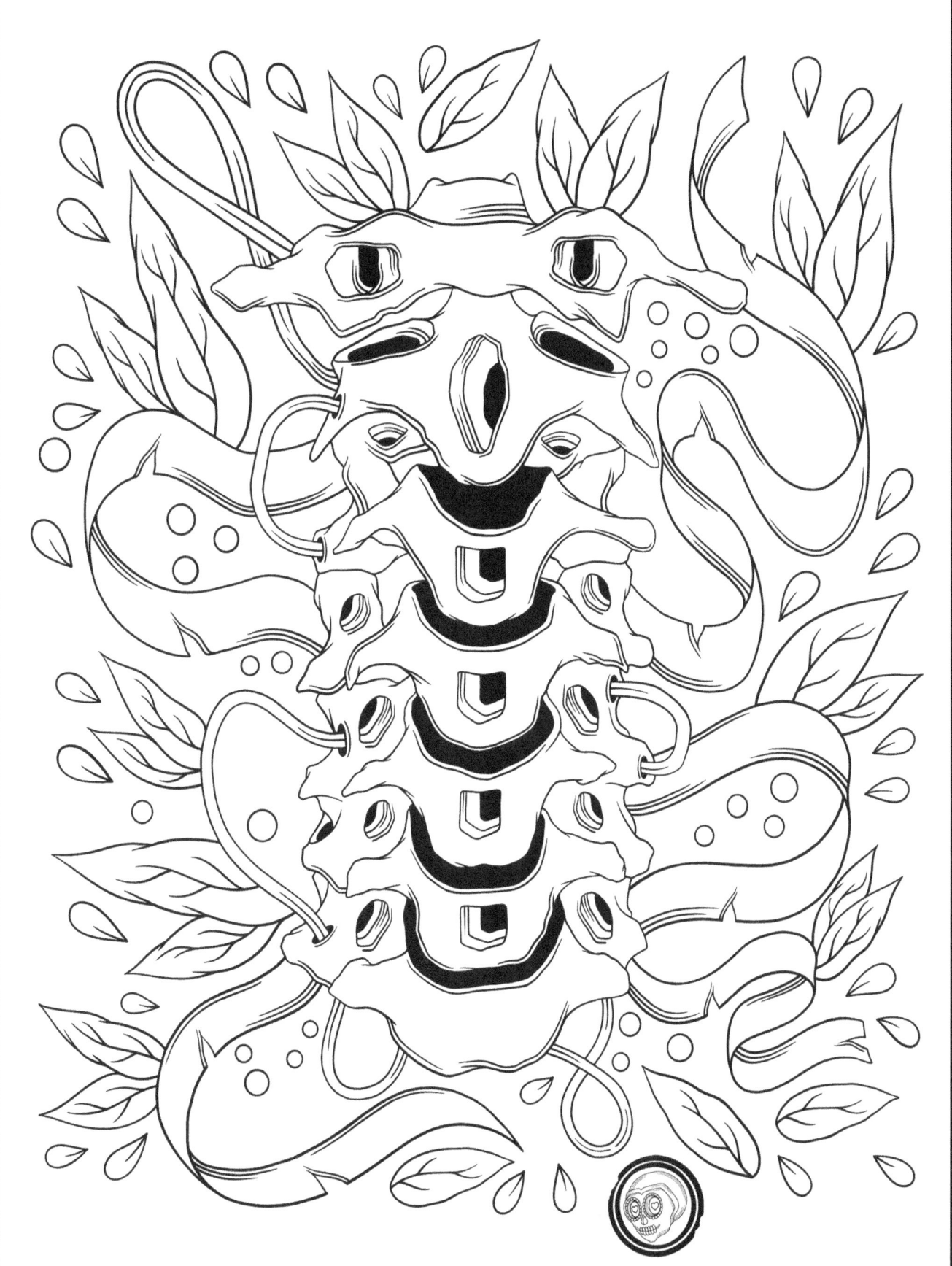

The Neck n Nature

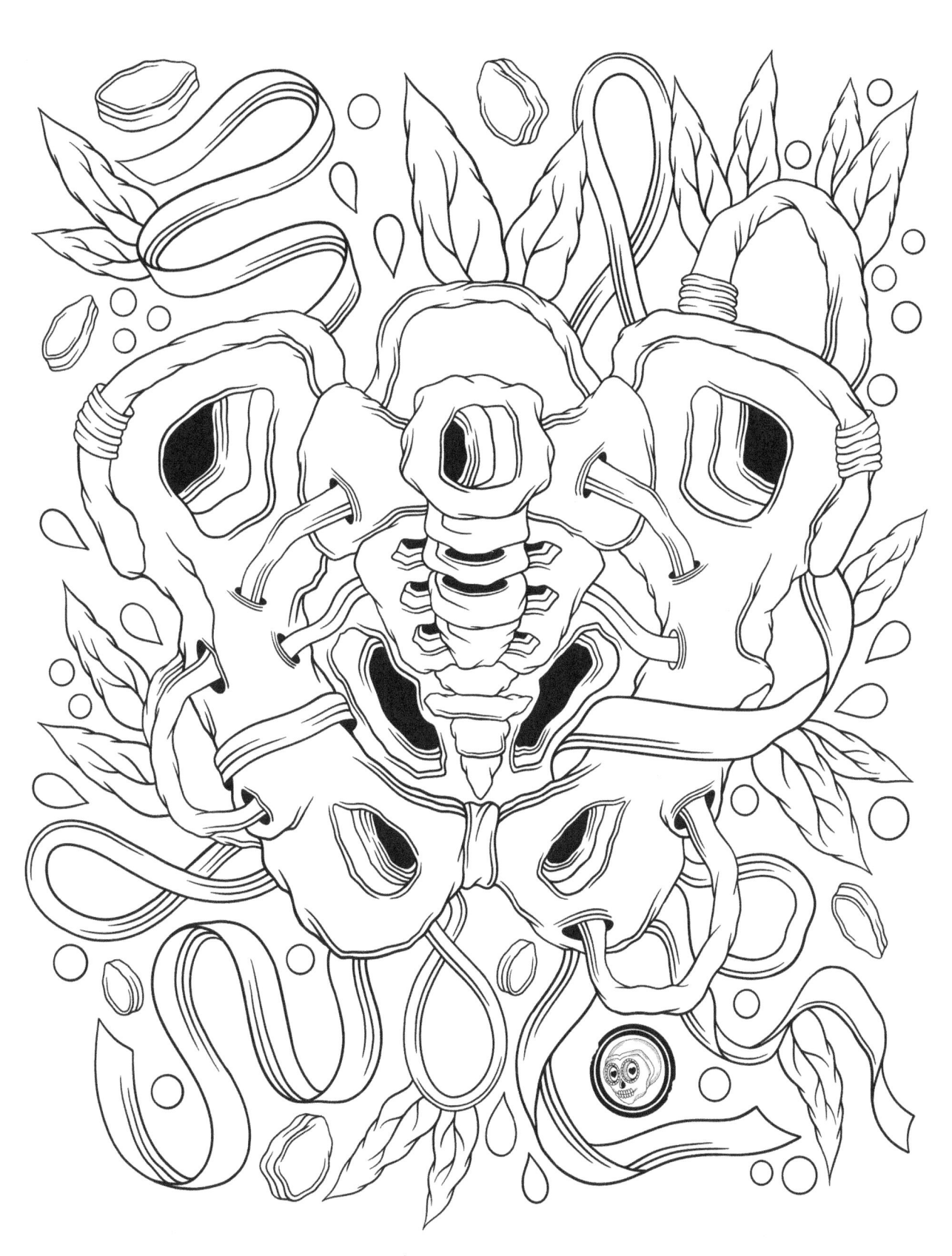

The Pelvic n Nature

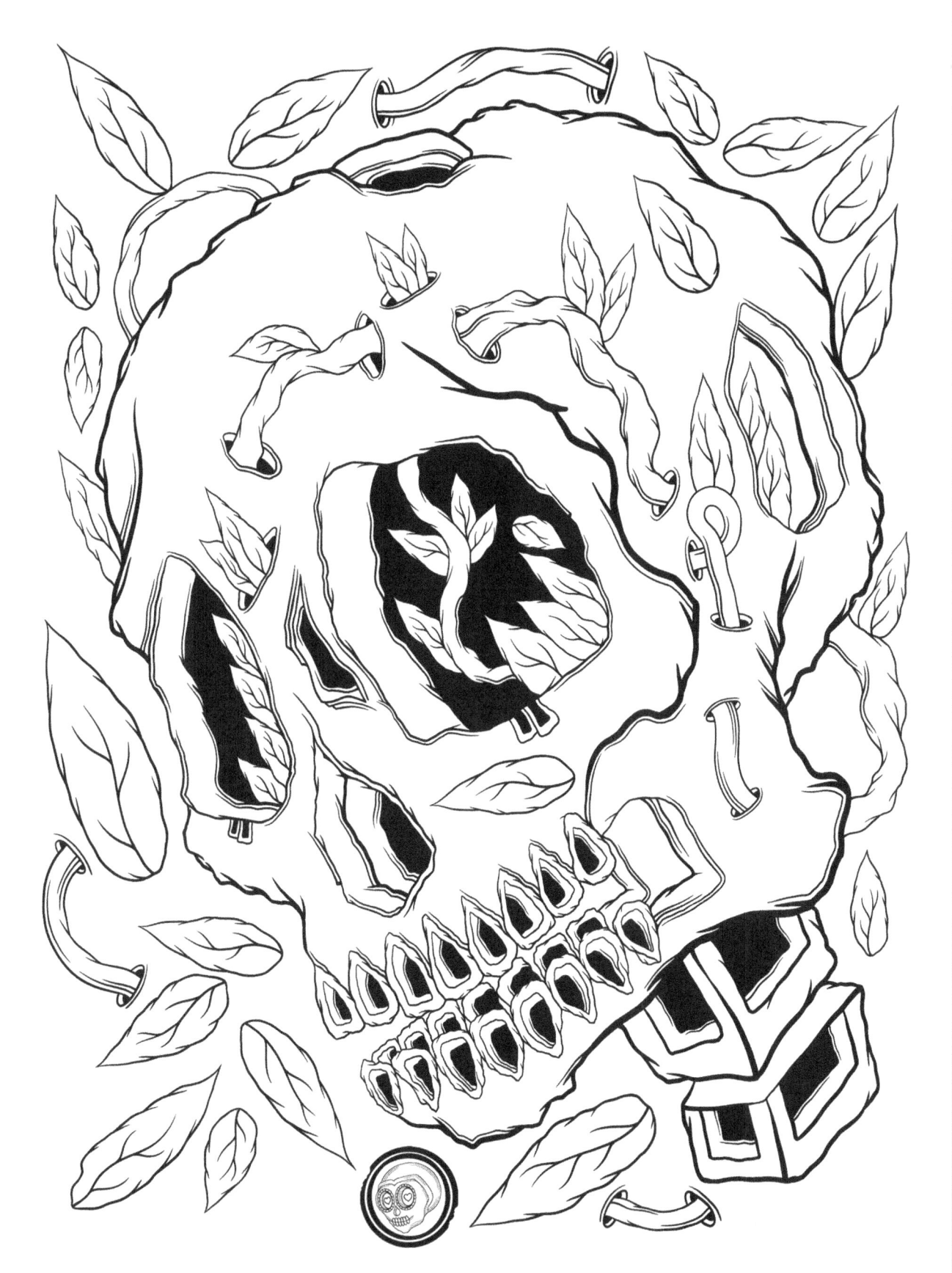

The Skull n Nature

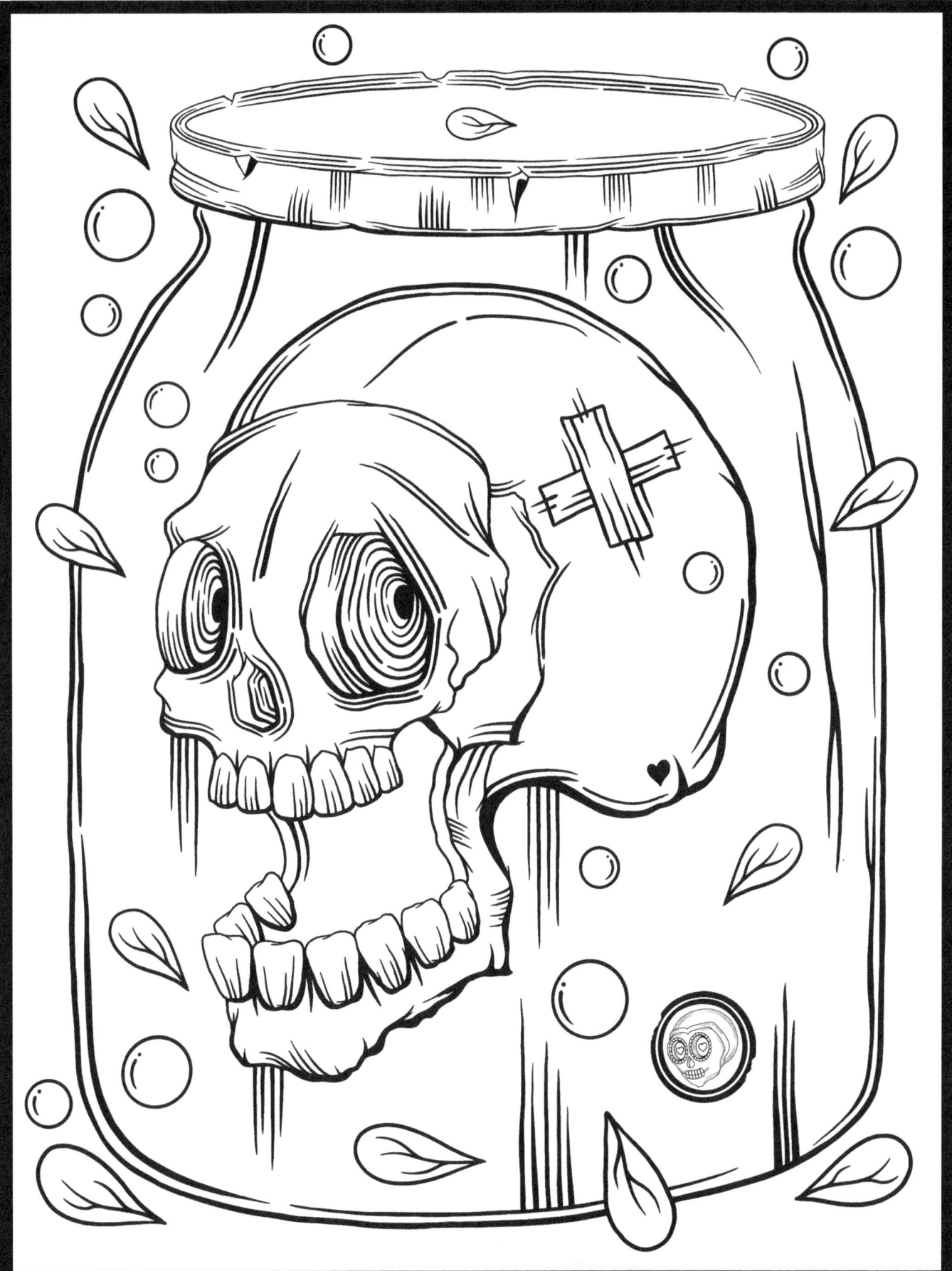

Keep it Fresh

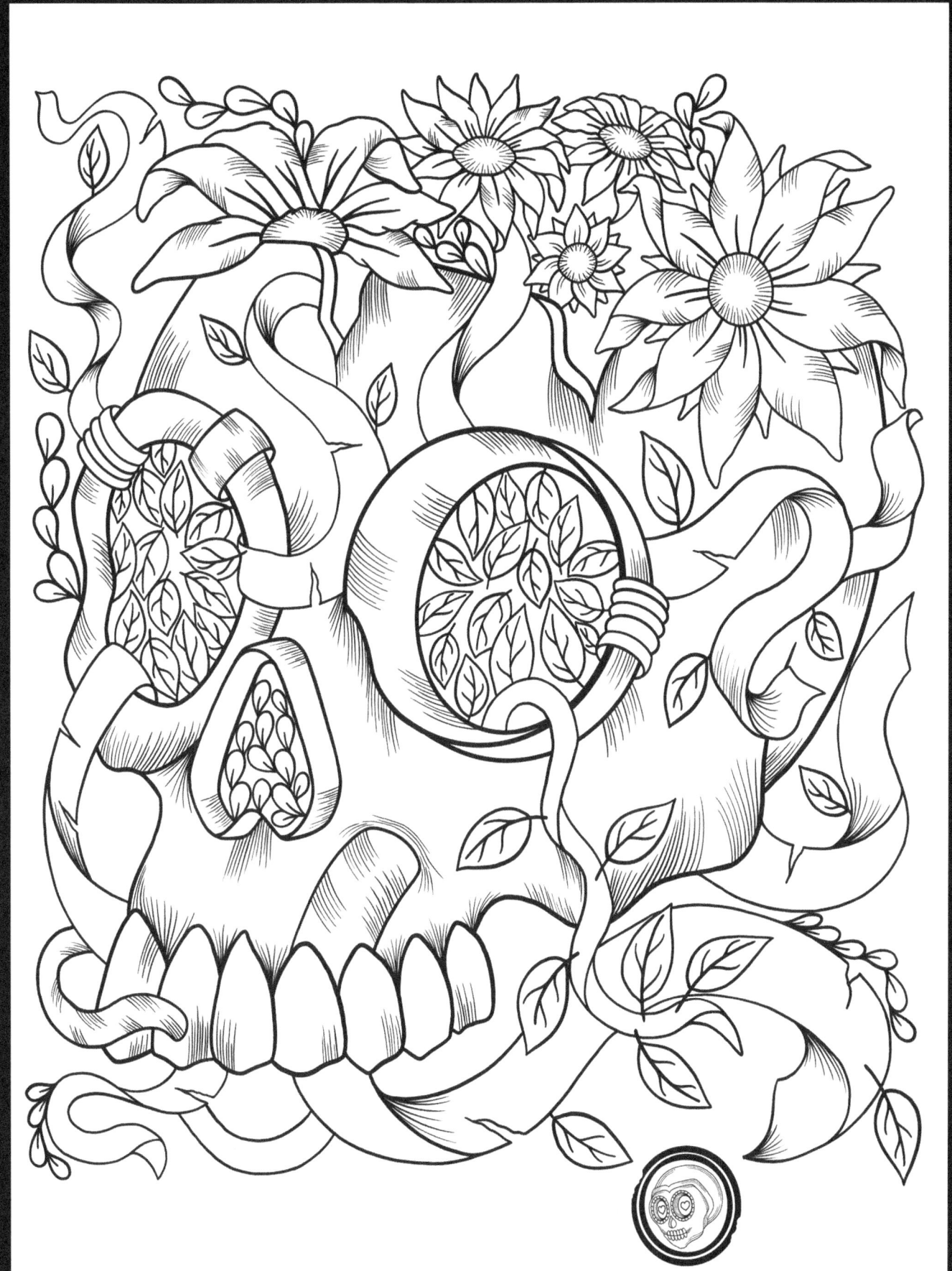

The Skull n Nature

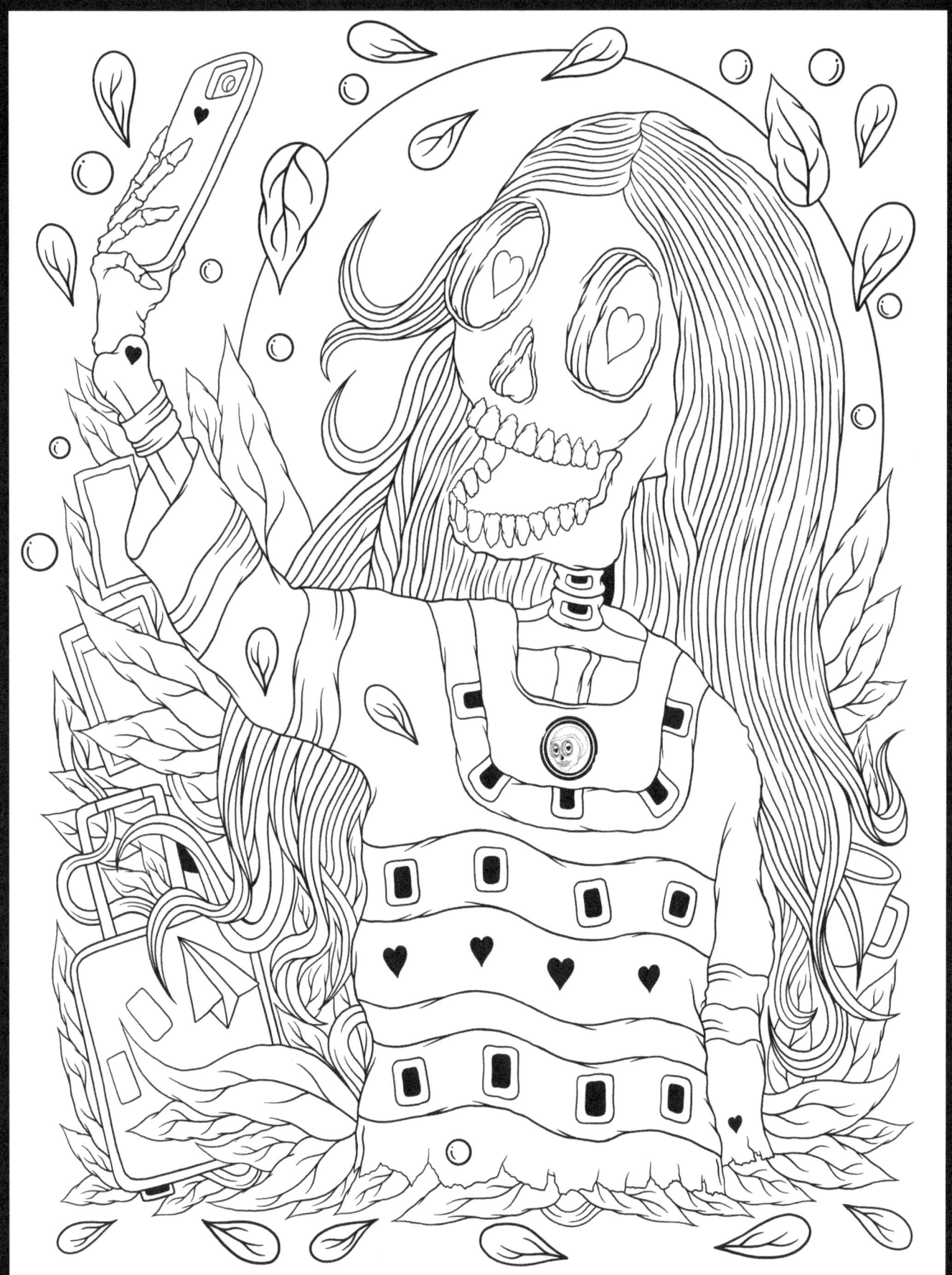

Selfie Time Smile

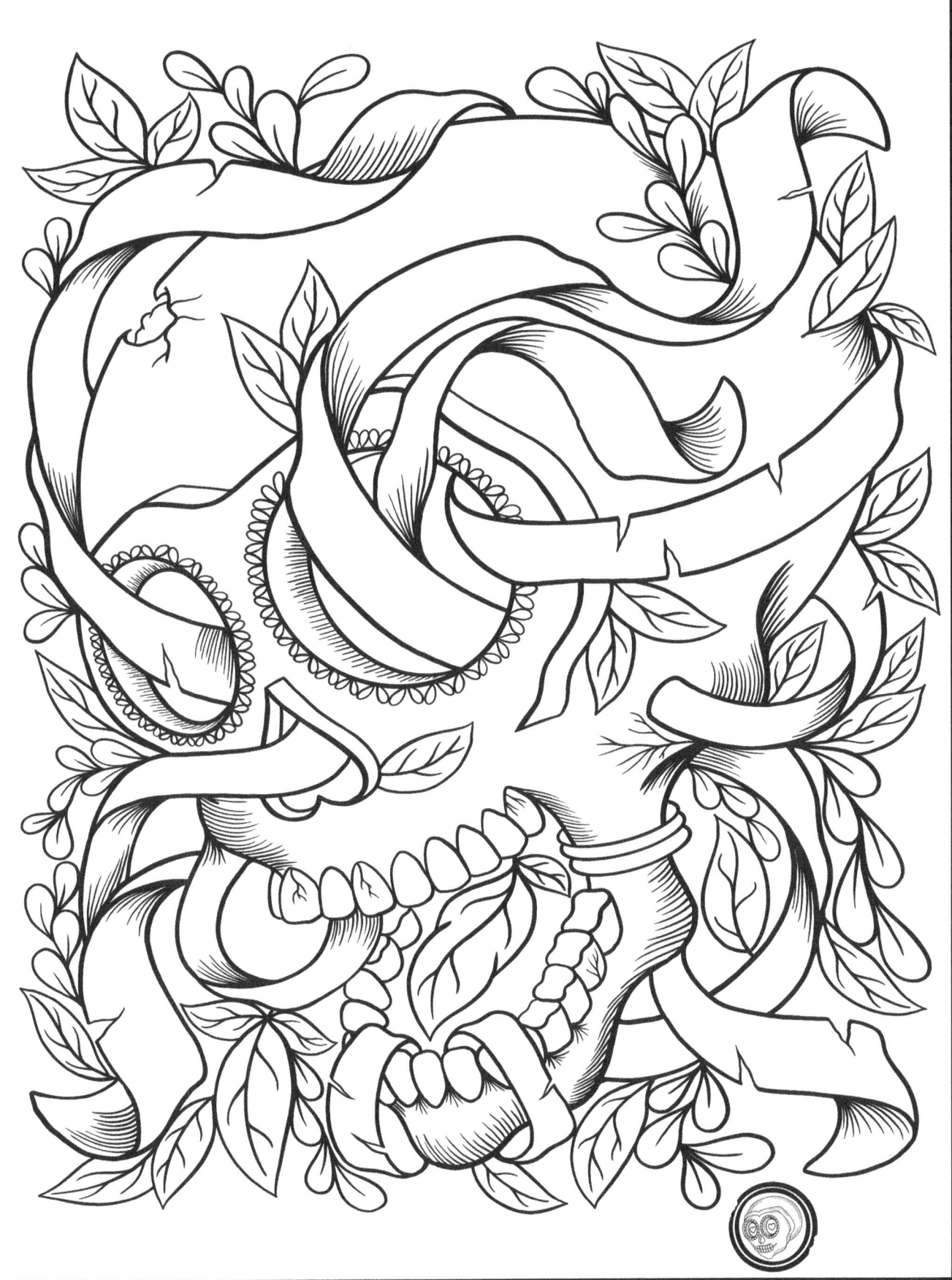

The Skull n Nature

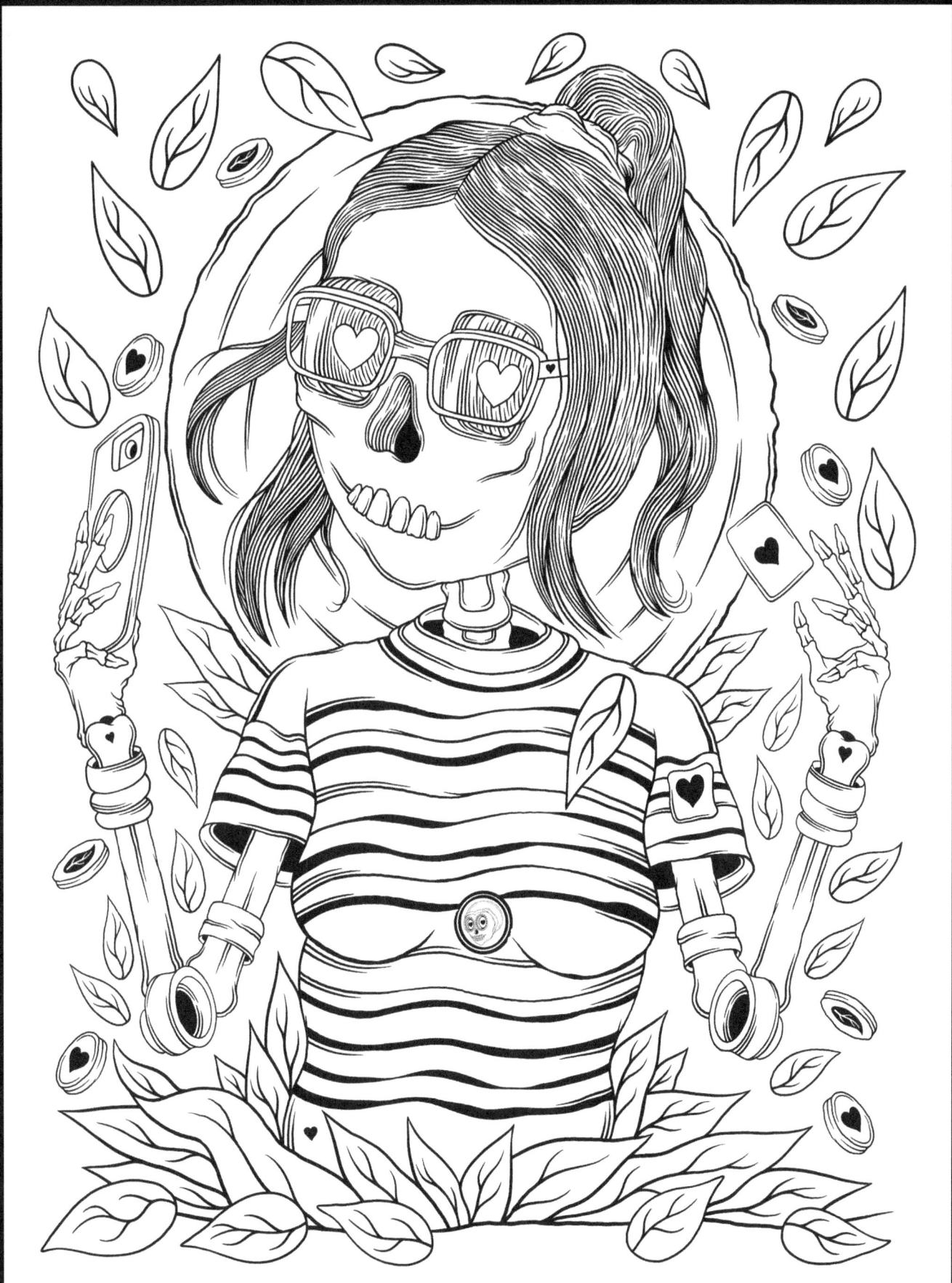

Mama's Day Off

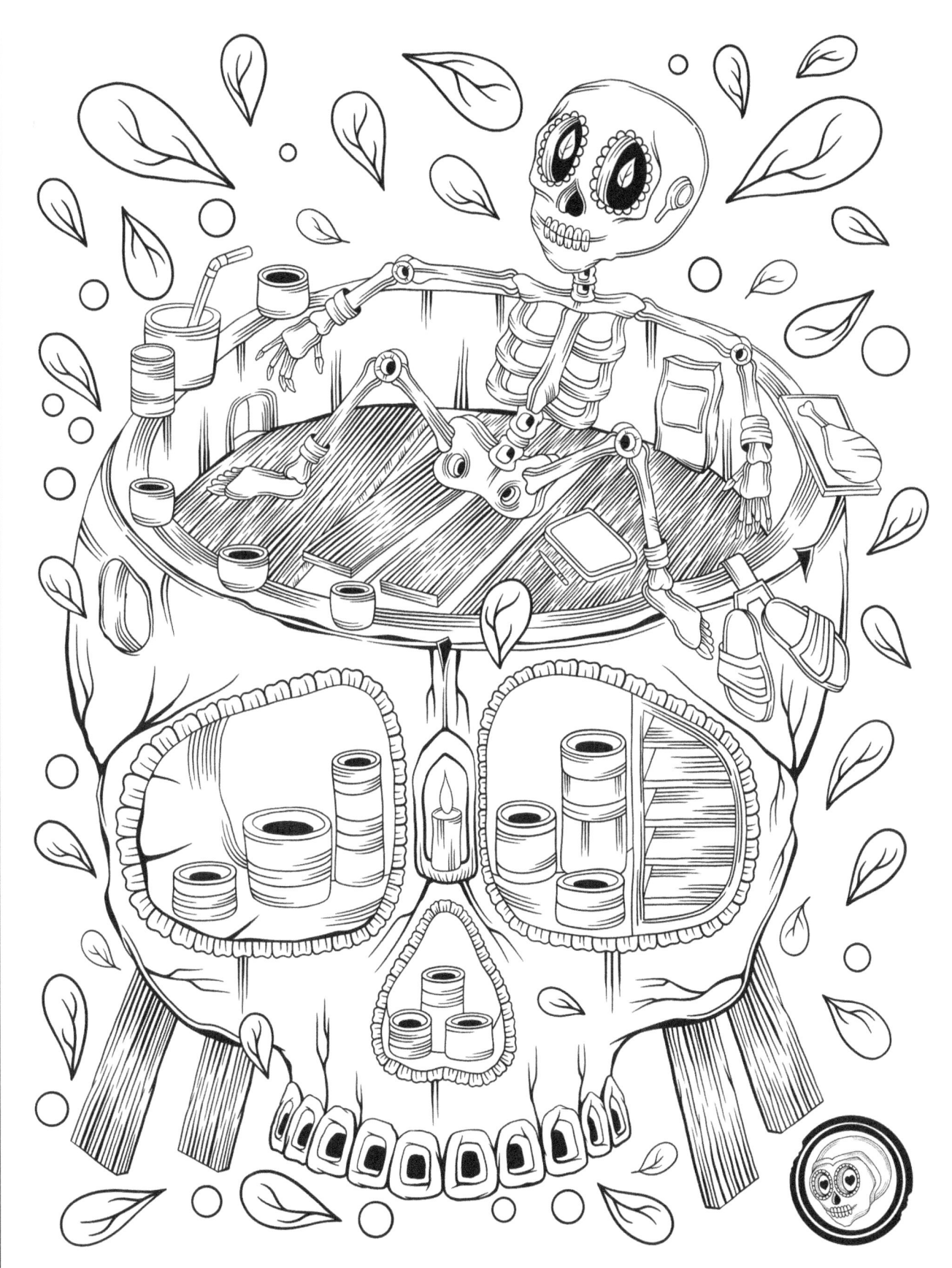

A Day Of Chillaxing

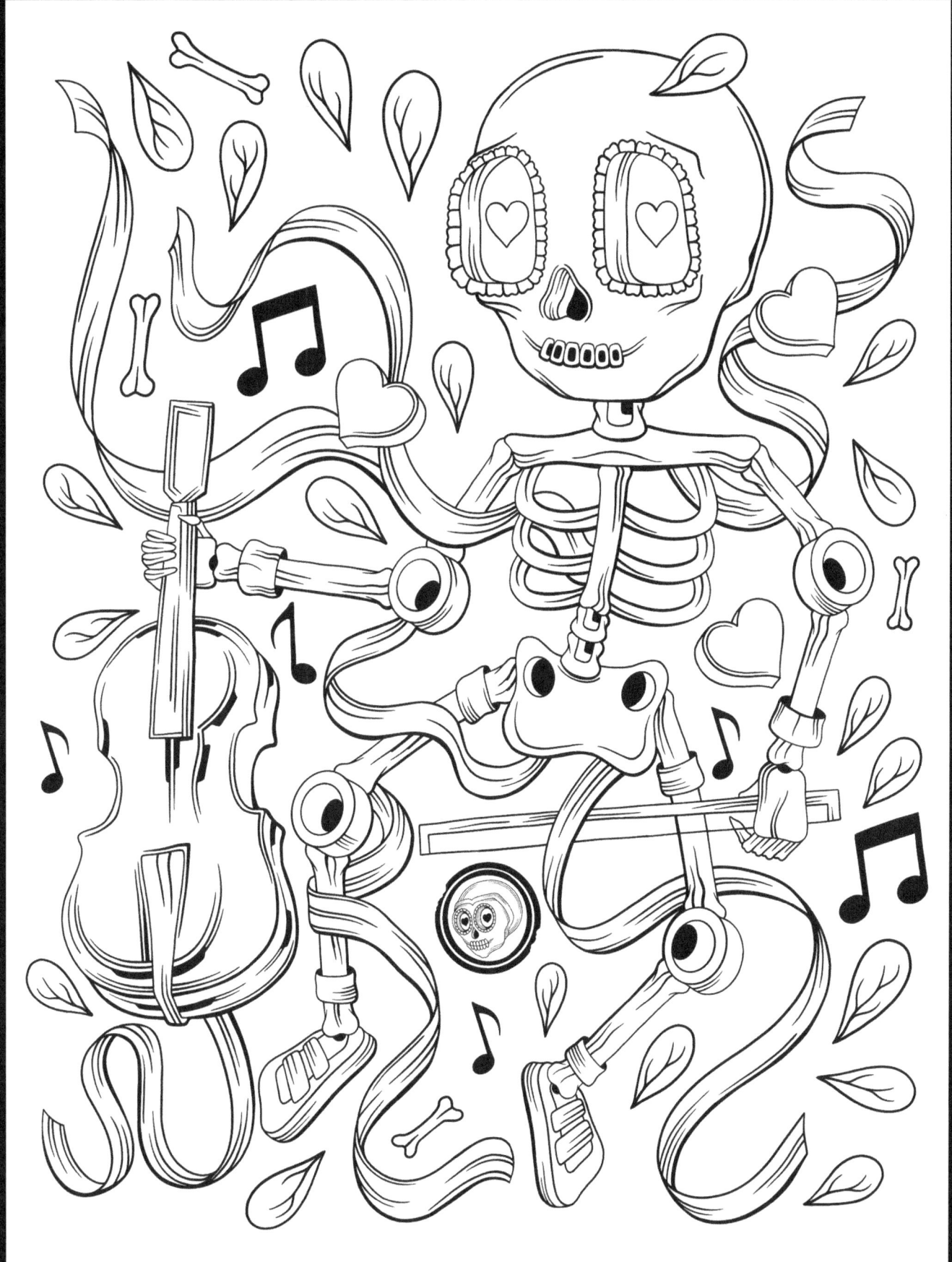

The Violinist n Nature

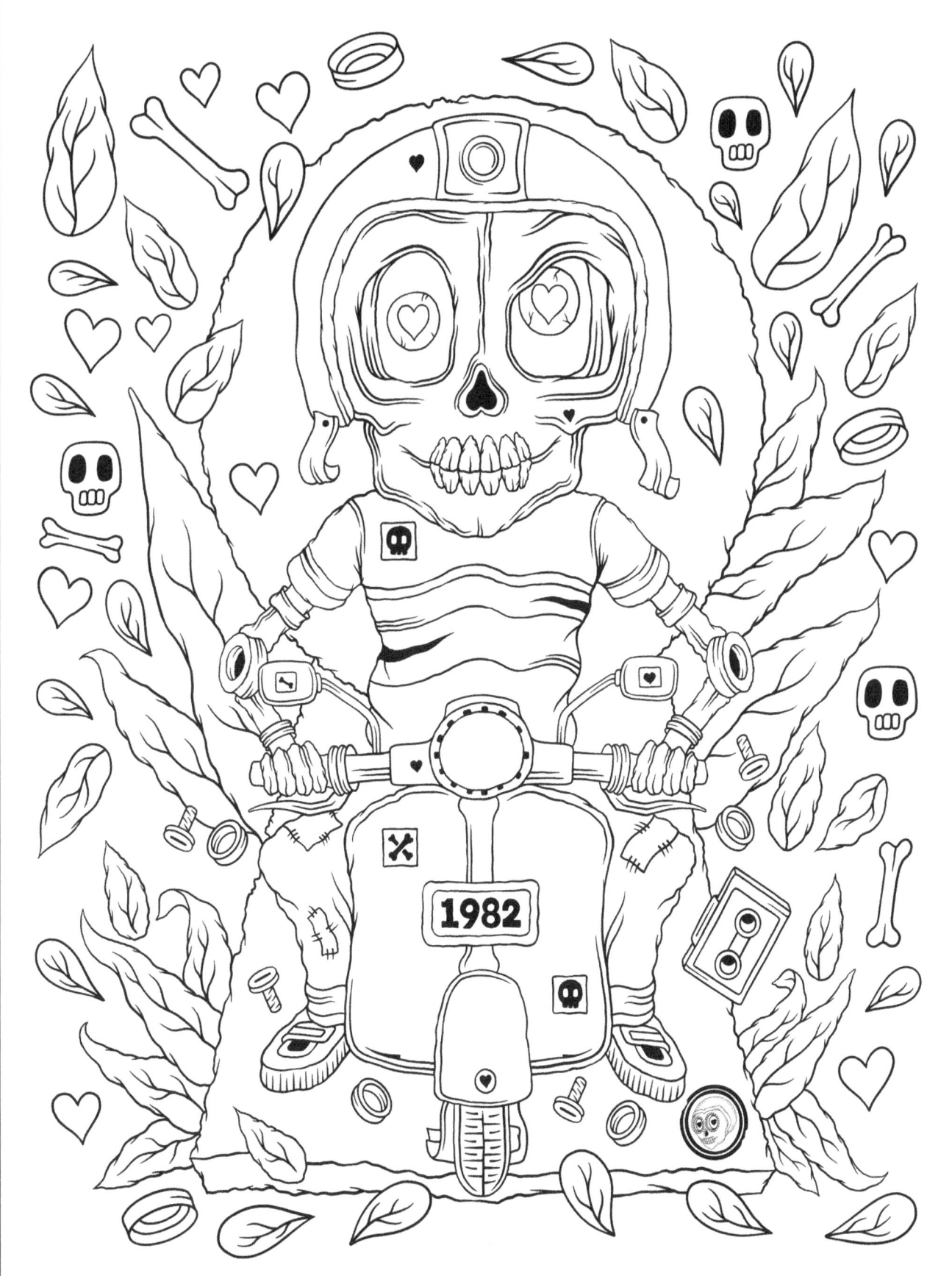

Let's Go For a Ride

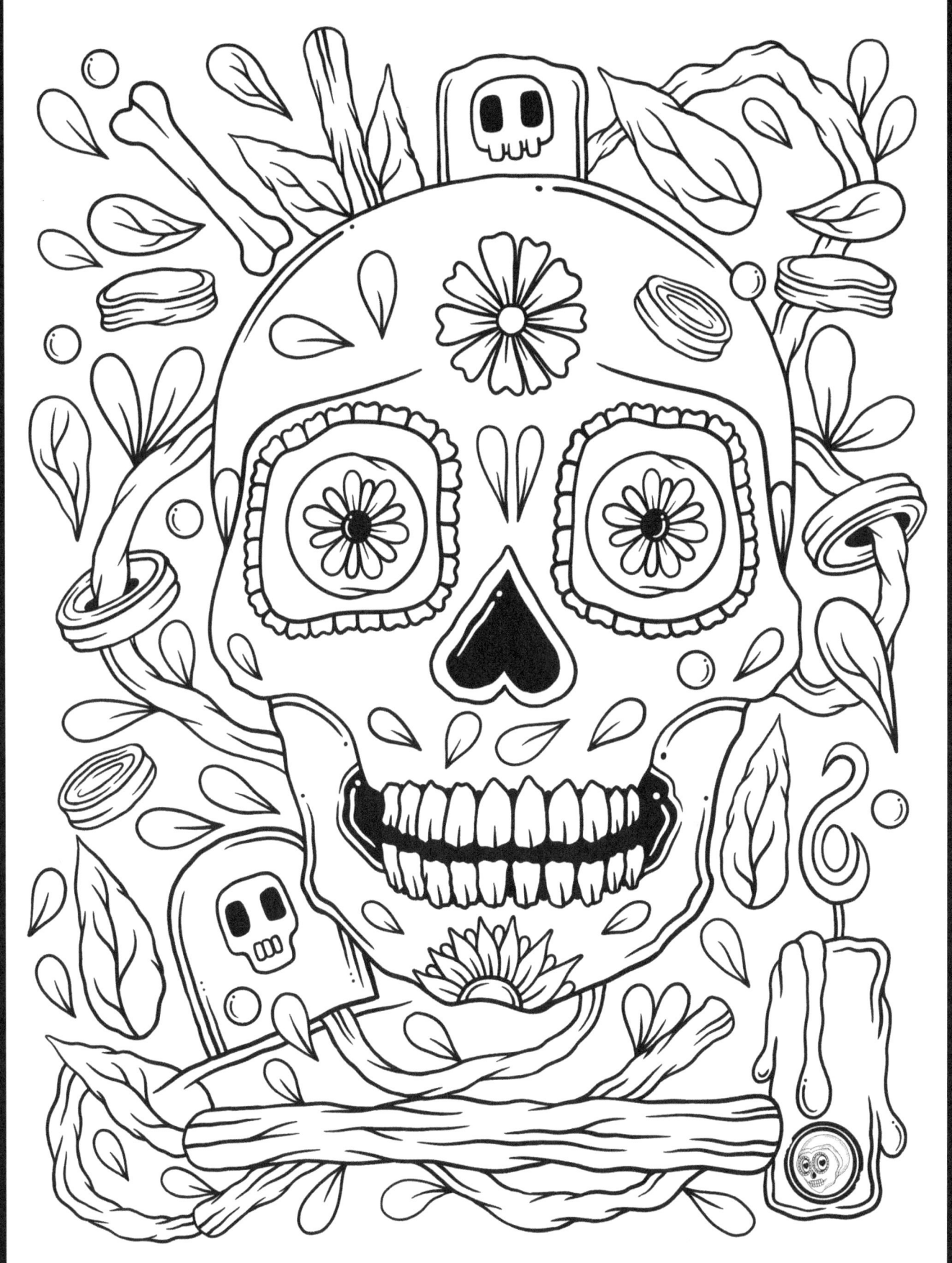

Nature's Surprise

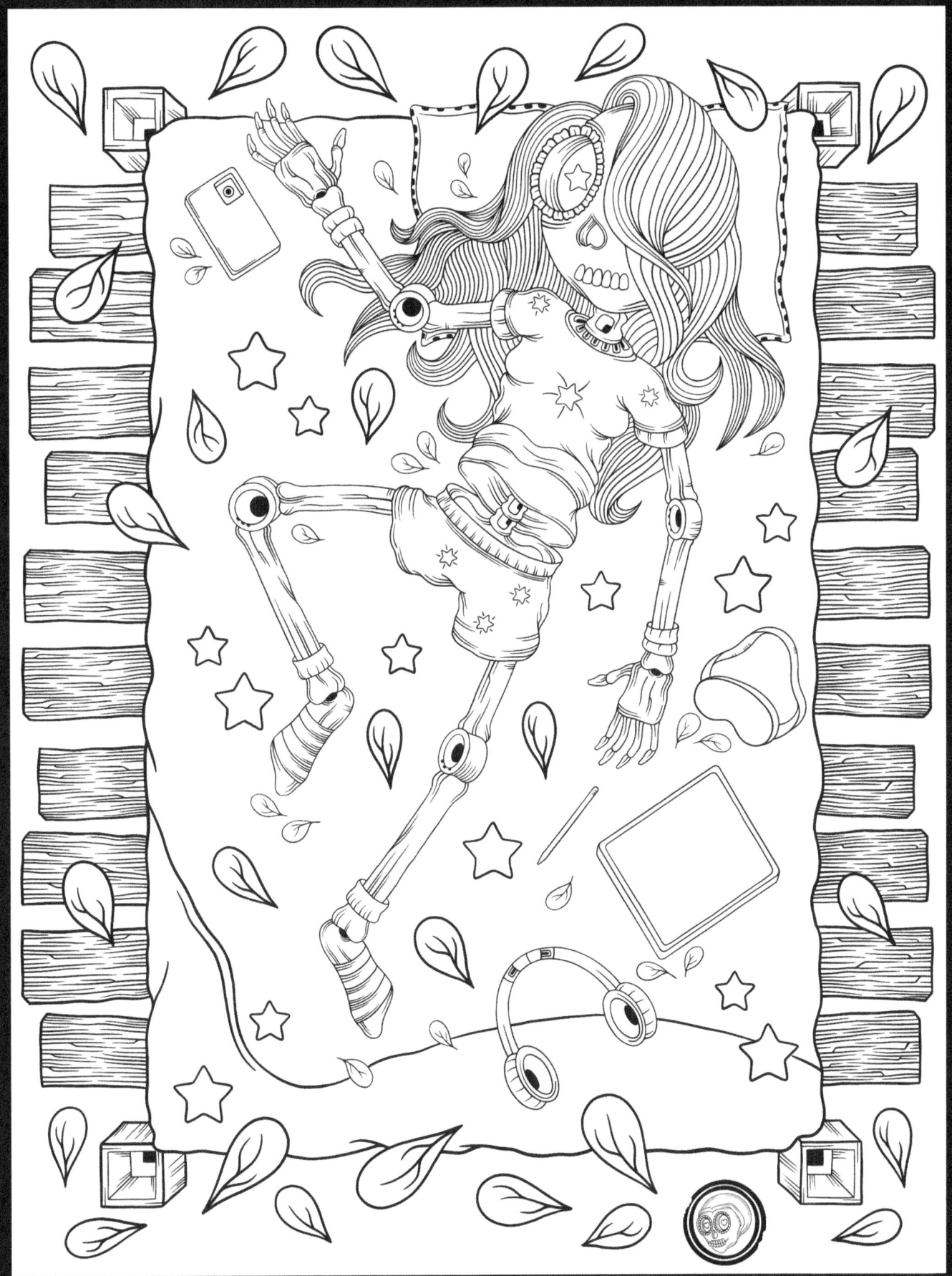

The Artist Dreamer

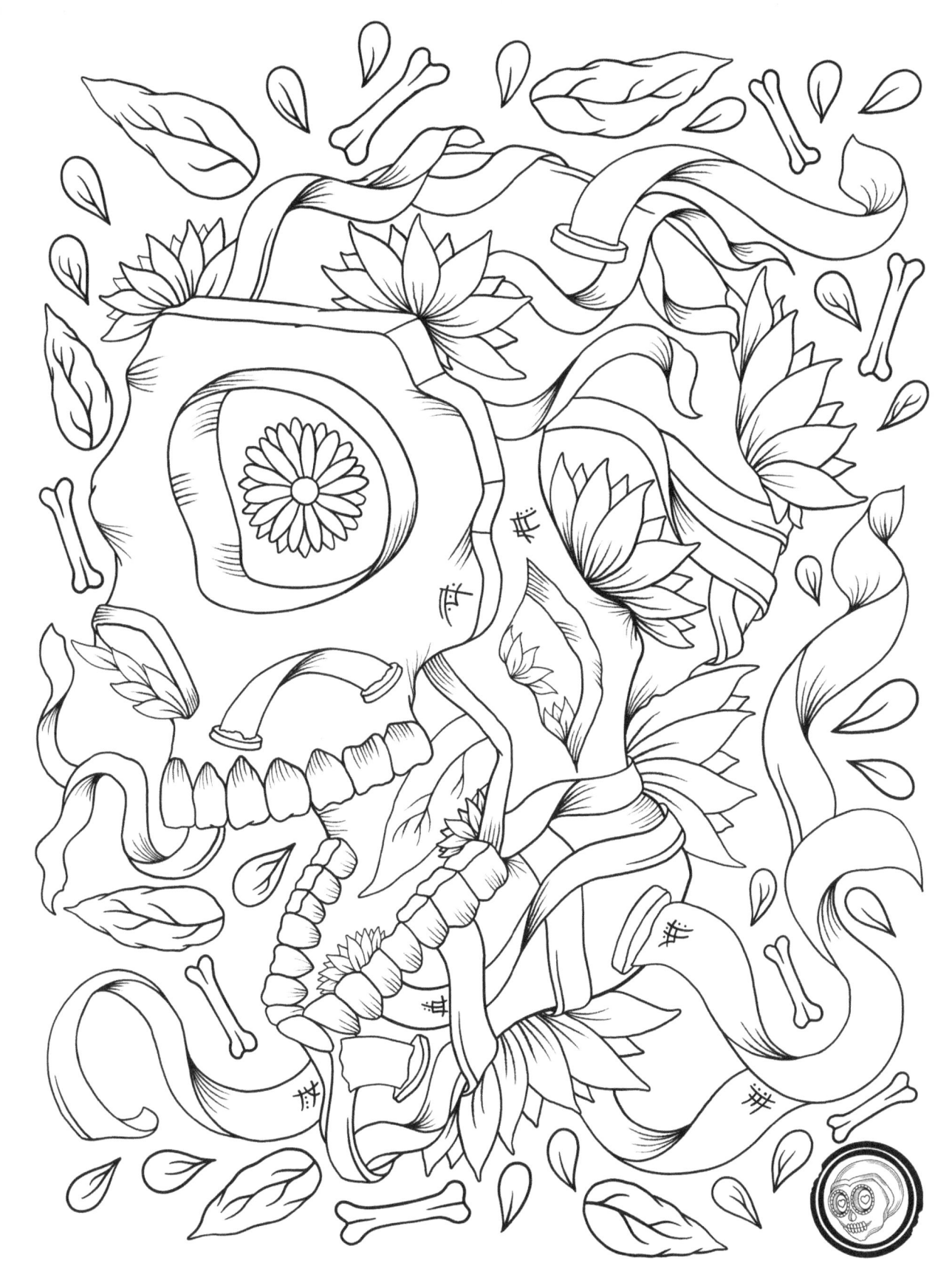

The Nature Lover

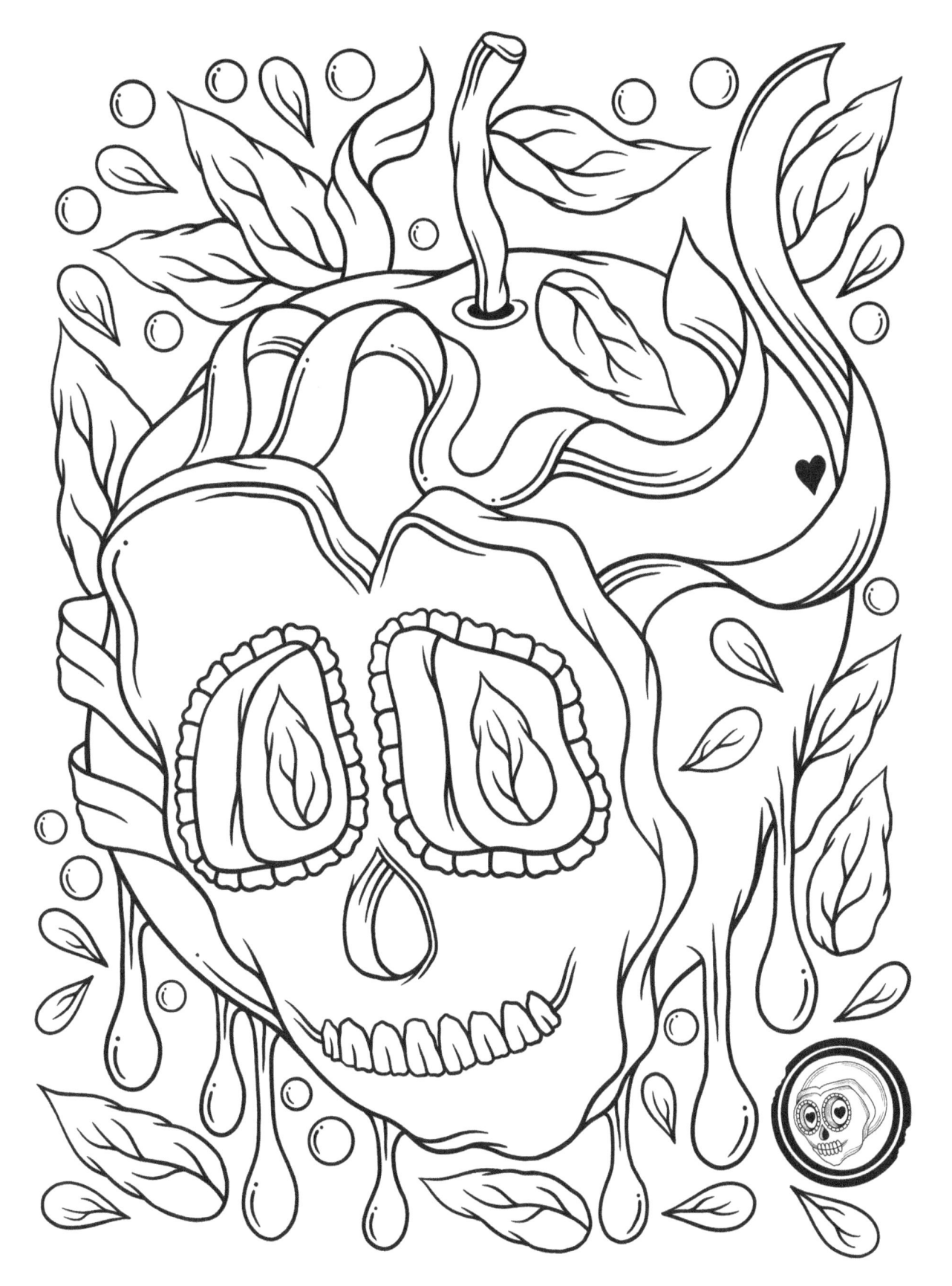

The Poison Apple

The Skull I.D.

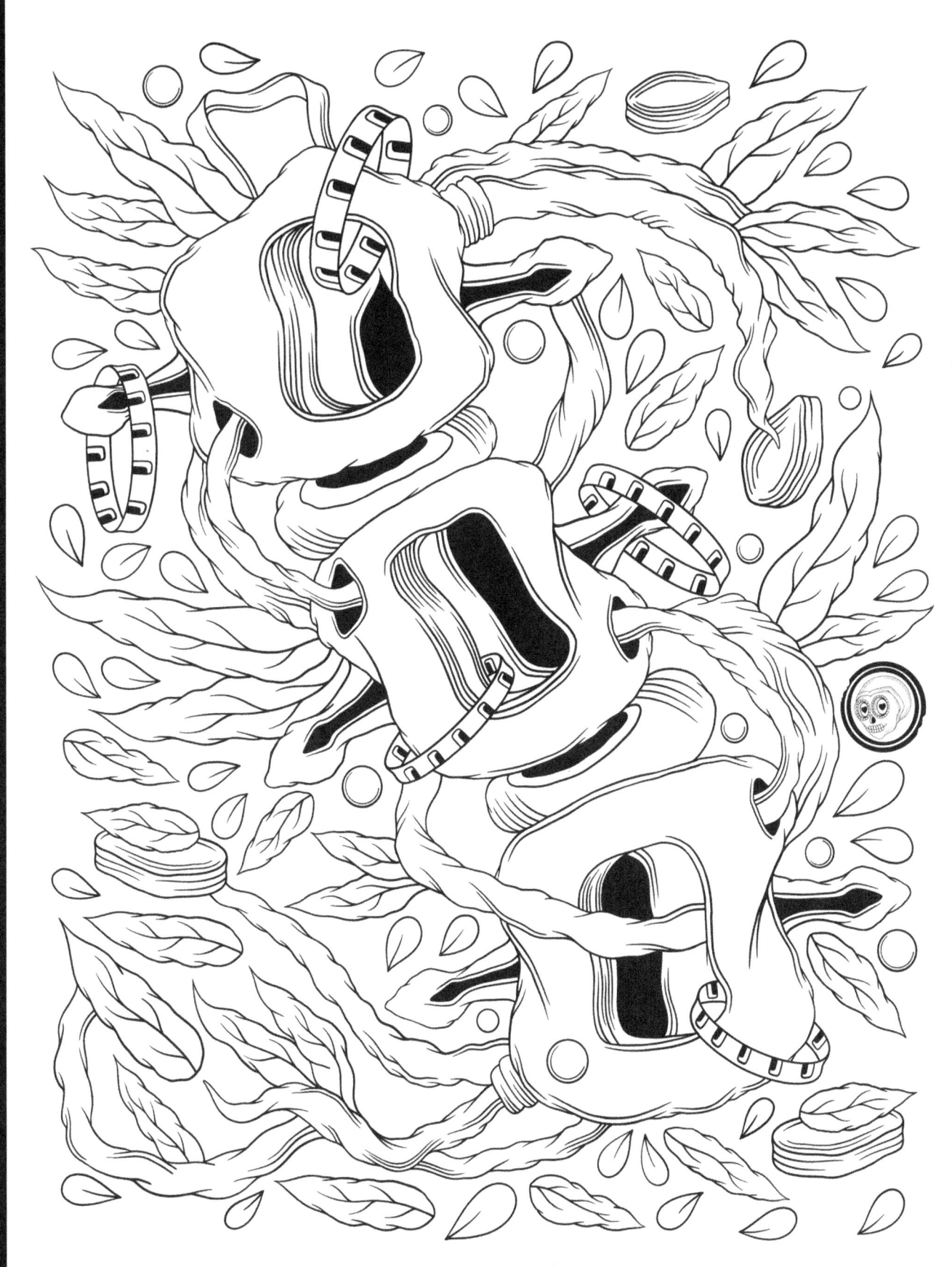

Twisted n Nature

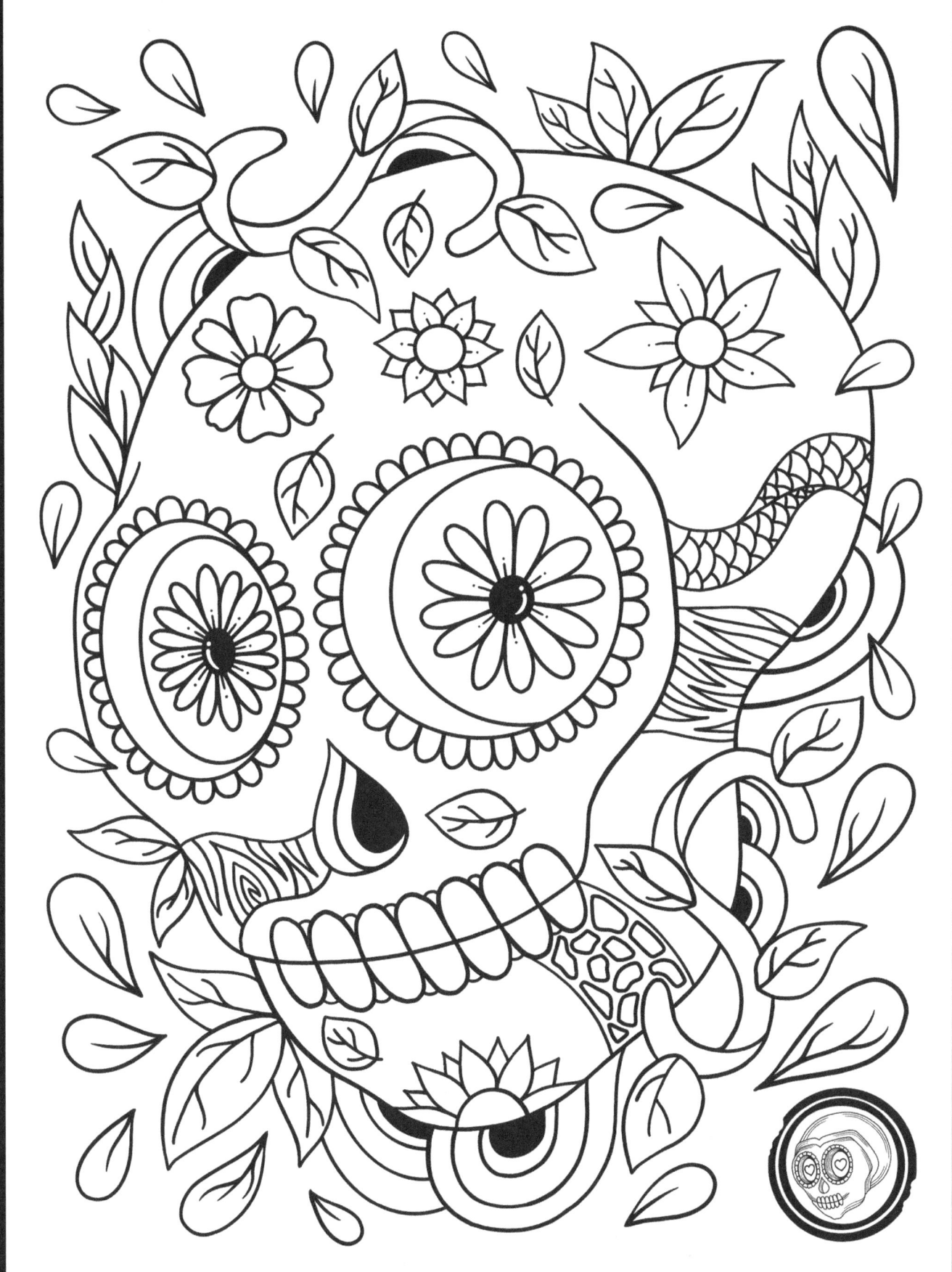

The Gardener

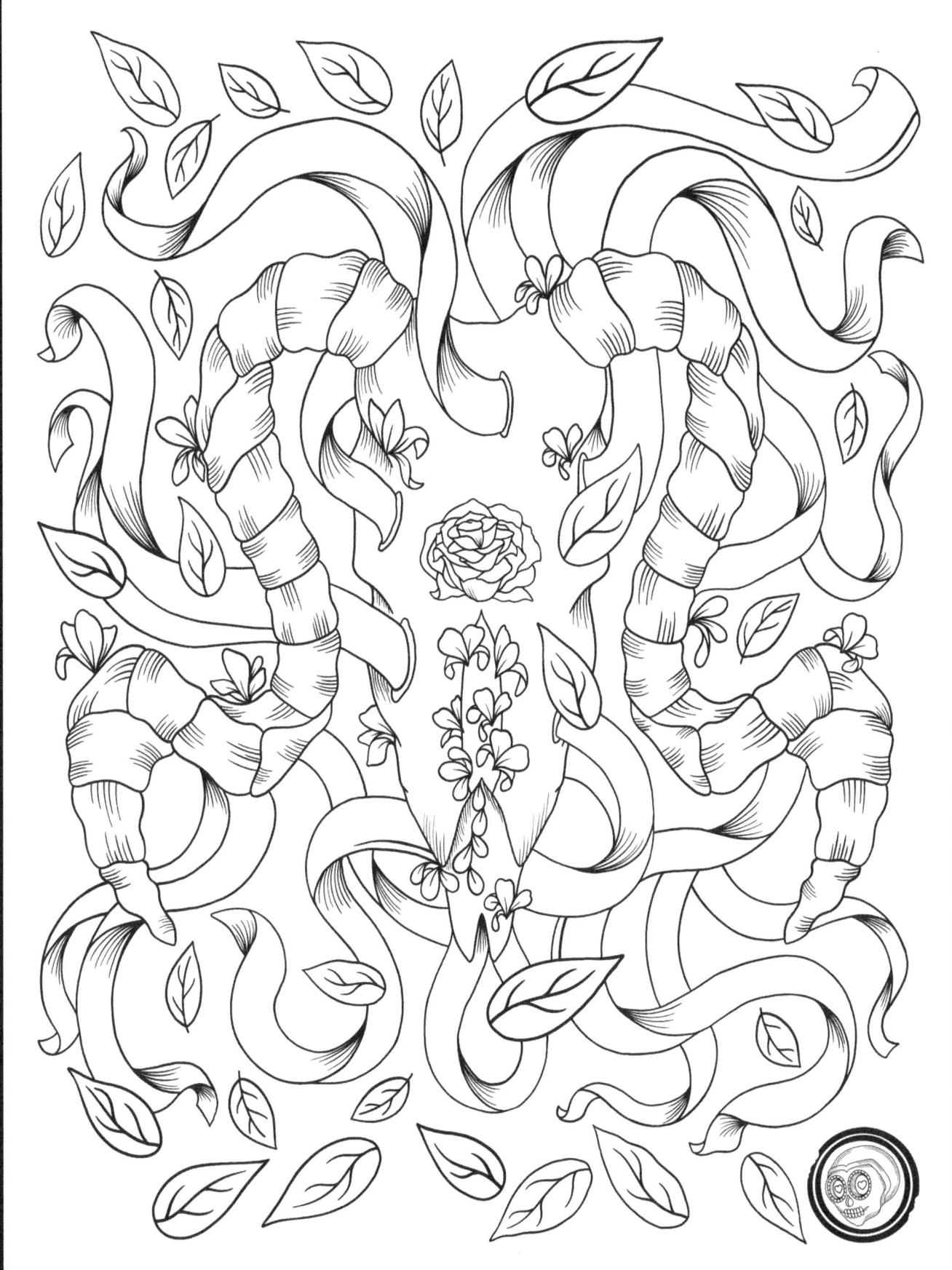

The Ram Horns n Nature

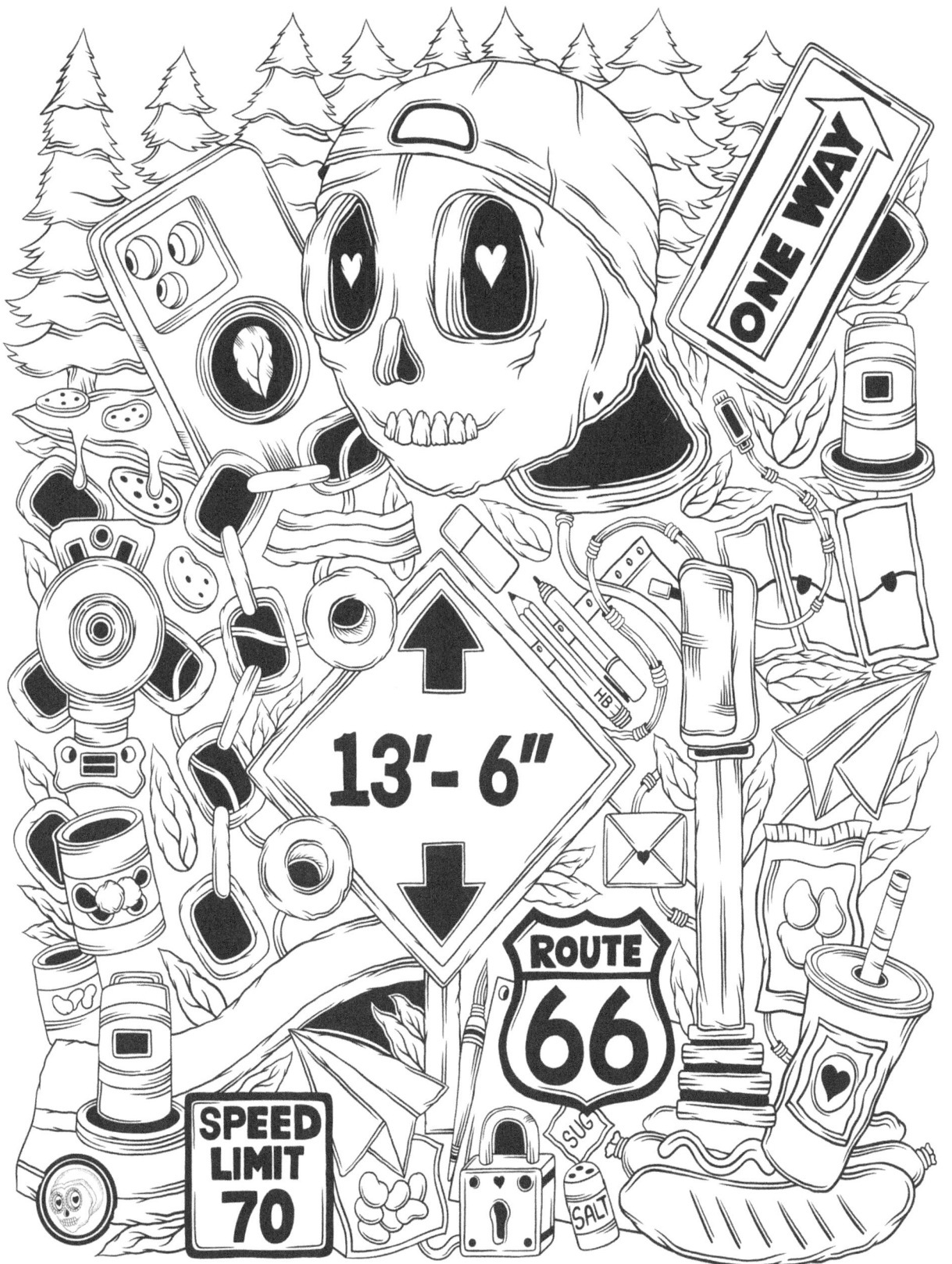

A Trucker's Story

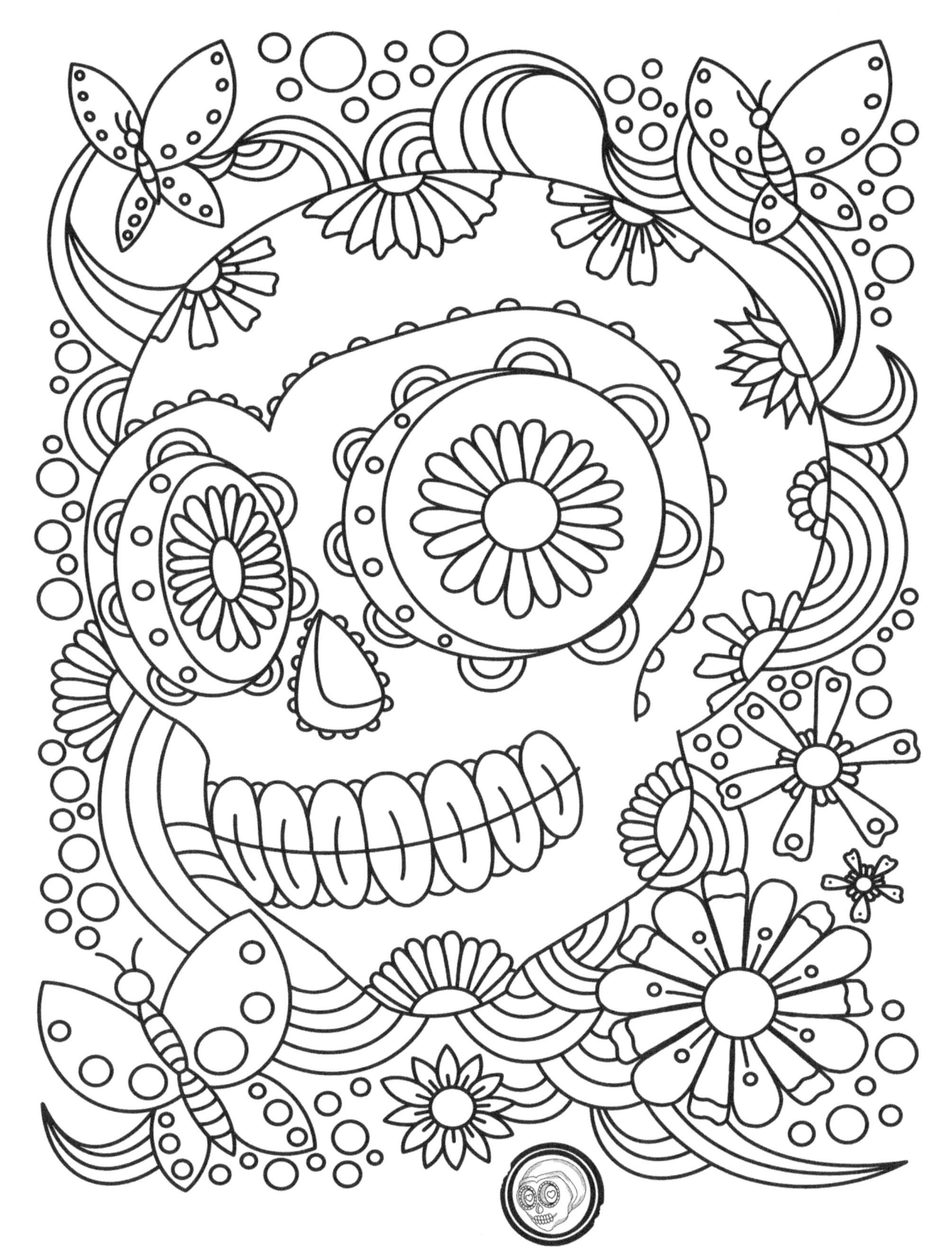

The Florist n Nature